STANLEY RYKER AND THE BIGFOOT RUN AROUND

KENNEY W. IRISH

HANGAR 1 PUBLISHING

STANLEY RYKER AND THE BIGFOOT RUN AROUND

Stanley Ryker and his two 3rd-grade best friends, Al (Alexandra) and Chunks (Jay) set out once again to save the day! While visiting their favorite summer camp, they are shocked to find that it may close due to numerous Bigfoot sightings. The 3 pull together to find answers and come up with a plan to capture the beast and save the camp. Stanley Ryker and the Bigfoot Run Around is a funny, empowering, quirky, fast-paced, edge-of-your-seat, what's-happening-next adventure!

CONTENTS

1

CAMP DAYBREAK

July!

Hi, I'm Stanley Ryker, but everyone calls me Ryker. I'm not sure why they use my last name, but I like it! I'm a soon-to-be detective...well when I grow up I mean. Certain things make me yell with excitement like summer, swimming pools, popsicles, and all kinds of stuff! I certainly love all months, but I have to say, July really might be my favorite month of the year...or maybe not. I can't decide. I can say that not having to go to stupid school makes it pretty awesome. I do have to say I miss my principal Mr. McCarthy. He's really cool! Anyways every year in July for three days and two nights, I get to do one of my most favorite things in the world to do! I love to go camping at Camp Daybreak.

Chunks and Al, my two best friends, feel the same way and they go for the same three days. They have two cabins; one for girls and one for boys. Oh, if you didn't know, Al is a girl. Al is short for Alexandra but never call her anything other than Al; she has been known to punch people in the face for calling her Alexandra! She's also the only girl I know who can climb a tree faster than me while in a dress.

By the way, never tell her I said that. I always say I let her beat me because she's a girl, and I'm just a good guy. Chunks (whose real name is Jay) got that well-deserved nickname in second grade when he blew chunks on the bus. On the other hand, he doesn't really climb trees as well as he falls out of them. Last summer, Chunks broke his arm and got twelve stitches in his forehead. It was kind of sad but kind of cool at the same time. I have to say, this summer at camp will probably be one of the best times yet! My mom dropped us off at camp, but the year before, we rode with Al's parents. When we got to camp, we met a camp counselor named Kyle. He was a skinny guy with really messy hair that always had a shine to it and always looked wet. Not really sure how he was able to get it to look that way all the time, but it was kind of cool, I guess. He wore the same hat everyday and kind of smelled like our gym at the end of a school day. Kyle waved his hands in the air and said, "Please, everyone, sit down!"

2

SCHEDULE OF FUN

W e all sat down on the grass, Chunks sat on my left side and some other kid named Jimmy sat on my right. Al sat with her group and her counselor Megan.

Megan had blue eyes and long brown hair. I have to say, I felt kind of funny looking at her. I think she's kind of pretty but maybe not...well, I guess for a girl maybe. My mom's really pretty, but she's a mom, not a girl, so it's not the same. I looked at Al, and she was talking with some girl I have never seen before. Just then, Kyle spoke up. "Welcome all young campers to Camp Daybreak." He continued, "These next few days, we're going to learn to kayak, build a fire with two sticks, and also learn how to swim." Swim, I thought, I love to swim.

I always jump off the high board at the town pool. Just then, Kyle said, "Thanks for sharing that with us." Oh man, I did it again! I sometimes say my thoughts out loud. Everyone just stared at me then Kyle continued. It seemed like forever, he finally stopped talking, and we went into our cabin. Chunks got in before me and ran to a bed, and I followed right behind. The rest of the boys piled in and chose the last few beds. My bed and chunks were side by side, which makes sense because we're best friends. Just then, Chunks pulled back the blanket on the bed and exposed the mattress. He just stared at it in shock. "Hey, what's wrong?" I asked. And that's when I saw—I saw the one thing no normal person would want to see in a bed they need to sleep in. No, it wasn't a spider, which would really stink having to sleep with one of those guys, and no, it wasn't a snake. It was bad, I mean worse than bad...I mean bad, bad...really bad. Right in the middle of the mattress was the biggest pee stain I had ever seen!

Chunks and I just stood there speechless. All the other guys gathered around and stared. It was quiet until that one kid, Jimmy, squeezed through and said, "Woo, that's the coolest, biggest pee stain I have ever seen. It looks like it's in the shape of a robot." Everyone agreed and began to laugh except for Chunks.

Just then, Kyle walked in and said it was time to go into the woods and discover nature. I'm not totally sure what he meant by that seeing nature has already been discovered, but I followed.

3

A GHOST STORY MAYBE?

There was certainly something different about Kyle, I said to Chunks as we walked out of the cabin and followed him to the beginning of a path that led into the woods. We all stood there wondering why we haven't gone in to discover nature, which has already been discovered and that's when we heard horrible screeching.

We turned around and there was Megan leading the girls right toward us. Another guy in our group said, "Oh come on, we have to go in with them?" Which was exactly what I was thinking. Just then, Al came running up to me and punched me in the arm and said, "Hey, jerk face." I have to say, for a girl, she has a mega punch. I did everything not to rub my arm but then I did, but I made it look like I had an itch. Al asked us how our cabin was. I laughed and said great. I could see in Chunk's face he didn't want her to know that he had a pee-stained bed. So like the good friend that I know I am, I looked at Al and said, "Chunks has a big robot-shaped pee stain in his bed." Al laughed and said, "Well, I guess we'll call you Chunks, 'the Pee Stain Boy." Chunks tried to think up a good come back all that came out was, "Yeah, well you're a pee girl." We just stared at him. I said, "What?"

Al just laughed and that's when Kyle and Megan spoke up and started to talk about our new discovery adventure. We followed them into the woods and continued to walk through the trail. We walked around for a while looking at tree barks and plants then walked back to the campsite. It was pretty boring, and I have to say, we already knew about tree barks. We all filled into the Mess Hall (cafeteria) to eat dinner. Not much happened for the next couple of hours or so, we just kind of walked around getting to know each other. Jimmy came up to Chunks and said, "Hey, I feel really bad about laughing at you earlier...if you want, you can have my bed." Chunks looked surprised; he smiled and said, "Really?" Then Jimmy burst out laughing and said, "No, are you kidding me?"

Chunks, I think, was about to tackle Jimmy when Kyle told everyone to settle down and to come out onto the beach. We all walked out together, the boys and girls, and when we reached the beach, they had wood piled up, and I thought, "Oh yeah, campfire!"

Kyle and Megan got the fire going, and we all gathered around it. We all just stared at the fire and enjoyed the sounds of the crackling wood as it burned.

Then Kyle looked up and said, "Guys, I don't want to scare anyone." Just then, I knew we were about to hear some cheesy ghost story, so I rolled my eyes. Kyle continued, "Has anyone heard of Bigfoot?"

4

THE LURKING BEAST

My eyes got really big, I have heard of Bigfoot. We just sat and listened as Kyle continued, "I myself went to this camp when I was your age, and one night, I was lying in my bed having a hard time going to sleep. I could hear the crickets chirping and then, for no reason at all, it became really quiet.

Then I heard movement outside of the window directly over my bed. I wasn't sure what it was, and I was afraid to look. I thought maybe it was just an animal or a branch rubbing the window. I wasn't sure, but I figured, it had to be one or the other. So I sat up and slowly looked out the window, and when I did, I couldn't believe my eyes. I was looking right into the face of a beast!"

Kyle shouted. "So big and so hideous I just dropped back down on my bed. I covered my head, and I didn't move a muscle. I was so scared, I didn't even get up to go to the bathroom." Just then, Jimmy looked at Chunks and whispered, "Now we know where the pee stain came from."

Chunks just scowled at him. Kyle continued, "And to this day, there have been many sightings that threaten to shut the camp down. So if you're in bed tonight and you hear something outside, I beg you, whatever you do...don't look out the window." Then Kyle just sat there quietly and didn't say a word. I started to think to myself. It was silent, eerie...then I looked at Chunks and Al and motioned to them to lean in. "I was thinking we need to come up with a plan to get the beast. After all, I do plan on being a detective when I grow up. Guys we need to come up with a plan to stop this Bigfoot." Chunks just looked at me and asked, "Why us? Why do we always have to be the ones?" Al just rolled her eyes and said, "If you love this camp, we need to make sure we do something."

We all walked slowly back to our cabins. We saw Al off and walked into ours. Chunks sat on his bed and didn't say a word, but I could tell he wanted to. So I spoke up, "Hey, I think that we really can do something here." "Like what?" asked

Chunks. I wasn't really sure but I had to do something. Every good detective comes up with a good plan. I brainstormed and that's when I remembered I saw some fishing nets hanging on the side of the building near the lake. "Hey, Chunks I think I know how we can catch the Bigfoot." Chunks just stared at me.

"Yeah, all we need is to grab the nets off the side of the building by the lake and sit up in the trees and wait for the Bigfoot to come by and we can drop the net."

Chunks asked, "Can we not climb the trees?" I then remembered how he falls out of trees. "Fine, we can be on the ground. When we throw the net on the monster we can jump on him and hold him down, and Kyle can call the sheriff. He'll take the Bigfoot away, and the camp will never have to close." Chunks didn't look convinced, but I have to say, he never does. I just said, "Let's get some sleep but also keep our eyes and ears open."

5

OUTSIDE MY WINDOW

We changed and lay in our beds, and I just stared at the ceiling. There were a bunch of cobwebs in the corners, which were kind of cool-looking, and moved every time a breeze came into the cabin through a window. I then closed my eyes and fell asleep. I'm not sure how long I was out, but I was awoken by a noise outside, and of course, it was outside my window. I looked at Chunks who was still asleep. I crawled out of my bed and over to Chunks. I poked him a couple of times until he finally opened his eyes. He started to talk out loud, but I quickly put my hand over his mouth and shushed him. His eyes got wide.

I said, "Hey, there's something outside, and I'm not sure what it is. I think it might be the Bigfoot." Chunks just stared into my eyes. I removed my hand from his mouth and he sat up. We slowly raised our heads up just enough so our eyes could peer out the window. We looked around but didn't see anything. We just sat there not sure if we should lie back down and that's when we saw a shadow that started moving across the ground. We quickly dropped to the floor and just sat there. We could hear something walk up to the window. We just sat there frozen and could barely breathe. Then we heard it move away from the building and walk into the woods. We didn't dare move just yet. A few minutes went by, and we agreed we should look out the window again. We slowly stood up and looked out and saw nothing but the moon. I looked at Chunks and said, "Wow, Kyle wasn't kidding, and we need to talk with Al first thing in the morning." Chunks agreed and we got back in our beds, and I don't think I ever fell back to sleep. Chunks was asleep in minutes.

The next morning, I jumped out of bed and woke up Chunks. Everyone else was still asleep. We quickly put on our clothes and ran out back and stood by the window we were peering out last night. Everything seemed normal, but I knew that we had to really look, any good detective knows that. We walked around the building and that's when we noticed the trash cans were knocked over and garbage was scattered all over the place. We just stared for a few seconds then realized what we were looking at. The Bigfoot had gotten into the trash looking for food! I looked at Chunks, and he stared back. We quickly dashed off to the girls' cabin to talk to Al and get her in on the plan for tonight. We looked in the window, but it was hard to see where Al was. I used my hands as a visor to block the morning sun from my eyes and could clearly see Al still asleep. I was just about to point her out to Chunks when all of a sudden we heard a voice yell out. "Oh gross, boys are looking in the window at us." Just then, all the girls sat up and saw us and began to scream. Before we could run, Megan came out in her pajamas and grabbed us by our arms, and dragged us back to our cabin. The girls were so loud it woke up the rest of the boys and Kyle. Megan dragged us into our cabin and did the worst thing she could have done; out loud she yelled, "These two boys were looking in the windows at us watching us sleep!" All the guys stared and laugh and point at us. I could feel my face get really hot, and Chunks looked like he was about to throw up, so I moved to the side just in case. Kyle smiled and told Megan he would take it from there. She gave us both a horrible look and stormed out. Kyle looked at us, and I thought we were toast. He quieted everyone down and told them to get dressed. He then took us by our arms and walked us outside. He sat us on a picnic table, Chunks and I on one side, and he sat on the other.

He again smiled and said, "Boys, I understand." I thought, understand what? Kyle continued,

"Guys, girls are really pretty." That's when I knew what he was about to say, I could feel my stomach start to ache. I yelled out, "No! No, they're not pretty!" Kyle just smiled and continued. I looked at Chunks who seemed to be very interested in what Kyle had to say. I rolled my eyes and tried to block out every word Kyle spoke. A few words made it through, but I survived. Kyle then told us we needed to clean up the building by the lake, which would usually really stink, but that's where the nets were that we needed. I thought, what luck!

6

THE PLAN IS THIS

W e quickly raced down to the building. Chunks tripped over his untied shoelace but somehow was not able to fall. Chunks spoke up and said, "Do you think the guys will make fun of us for looking in the windows of the girls' cabin?" I thought for a moment and said, "No, I don't think they will—I know they will." We just stared at each other then started picking up and moving around the camping gear in front of the building. It was starting to get hot out, and we began to sweat. I was just about to take my shirt off when I heard, "Hey, jerk faces."

It was Al, and she came over and punched us both in the arm. "Hey, I heard you losers were looking into our cabin this morning." I was just about to tell her what happened when I looked at the net hanging on the side of the building. I leaned in and said, "Hey, I have a plan to catch the Bigfoot." Al's eyes opened wide. I really think Al thinks I have good plans, but for a girl, she comes up with some pretty good ideas herself. I pointed to the net and Chunks, and I told her about the night before.

Al asked, "Did you find any footprints?" Boy, that girl was a smart cookie. We never even looked!

I said, "No, but we did find some trash cans knocked over so we believe he was in them." We decided we would pull the net down and hide it in the bushes behind our cabin for tonight. Al helped us pick it up and quietly carry it to the back of the cabin and hide it in the bushes. I pointed to the window we were looking out last night, and Al just put her hands on her hips and stared. I'm not sure what she was thinking, but whatever it was, she just stared at the window. Then she spoke up, "if the Bigfoot was looking into the window at Kyle when he was a boy, it really must be super big...nine feet tall maybe?" She was right...I then spoke up,

"So tonight, after everyone is asleep, we'll meet out here around ten p.m. and wait in the bushes for the beast to come by. When it walks through the path behind the cabin, we'll throw the net on top of it and yell, so Kyle and everyone will come out

and help us." In my mind, it kind of sounded like a good idea, but it's all I had.

We agreed to the plan and ran back down to the building by the lake and finished up arranging the supplies. Al went back and hung out with the screeching girls. It took a few hours, but when it was done, it was done. Before we knew it, lunch was being served, so Chunks, Al, and I sat at the same table and continued to talk about tonight.

We looked at it from every angle and came up with some ideas in case it didn't go as planned. Just then, Jimmy came over and sat with us. "Hey, you, peeping toms," he called us. Chunks again looked like he was going to tackle him. I quickly spoke up and said, "That's not what we were doing. We were looking for Al." Chunks then spoke up and said, "Yeah, we needed to talk to her about our plan for tonight." Al and I just stared at him with our eyes wide open.

Jimmy smiled and said, "I knew you were up to something, and whatever it is, I want in on it." Al yelled, "You can't." and gave him the meanest look she could.

Jimmy said, "Okay, no problem, I'll just have to talk with Kyle about it." Before he could say anymore, I said, "Fine, you're in, but you can't say a word to anyone." Jimmy agreed, and he leaned in, we let him in on our plan to catch the Bigfoot and save Camp Daybreak.

7

WE GOT HIM!

The day continued on, and we went out in a few boats. Al had to go with her group, and Chunks, Jimmy, and I went in the same boat. We looked around the lake, and I could smell the dampness of the life jackets we were wearing. The lake was quiet and pretty much motionless. A few waves rocked the boat every few minutes, and the sun, every once in a while, hid behind the clouds. I looked over across the lake and that's when I noticed something moving in the woods. I motioned to the guys to look over at the same spot. We just sat staring at the woods. You could see a figure moving around. I thought maybe it was just another camper. Where were they camping...the only camp on the lake was Daybreak.

Then before we knew it, the figure was gone. Jimmy looked at us and said, "Wow, that had to be Bigfoot." Chunks agreed.

Not long after, Kyle was yelling at us to paddle back into shore. We grabbed our paddles and made our way to the beach. We did a few more activities throughout the afternoon like swimming and carving animal shapes out of blocks of wood. I made a dog but it looked more like a beat-up block of wood than anything. Soon, it was time to eat dinner, and Al sat with us. I looked at Jimmy and said, "You better not freak out and run off!" Chunks backed me up and said, "Yeah, you can't ruin this, it may be the only chance we have to save the camp." Al spoke up and said, "If you screw this up, I'll deck you." Jimmy's eyes opened wide and assured us he was in and was going to do his part.

We finished eating and then helped clean up the mess hall. It wasn't long after we had to go to our cabins and get ready for bed. Al left us and went with her group, and Jimmy, Chunks, and I sped off to our cabin and washed up, and got into our beds. We agreed we would all keep eye contact with each other, and as soon as ten p.m. came, we would quietly sneak out and meet up with Al. It seemed like forever as we lay there. It was quiet, and you could see we were all scared, but we knew what we had to do. Finally, ten o'clock came, and I slowly got up. I could see Jimmy sit up, but Chunks didn't move. I couldn't believe it, he had fallen asleep. I crawled over to his bed and poked him a few times. He opened his eyes, and I quickly put my hand over his mouth, so he couldn't speak. I whispered, "You fell asleep! You could have ruined the whole thing." Chunks apologized and he, Jimmy, and I crawled across the floor and quietly opened the door and crawled out of the cabin.

We hurried around back to where the net was, and Al was already there sitting by a tree. She looked at Jimmy and smiled and said, "I guess you're not a total doofus. I thought for sure you would back out." Jimmy scowled at her and said, "I gave you my word." I shushed them and motioned them to get ready. We each grabbed the net and ducked down and waited. I could see on Chunks' face he was really scared, but I have to say I probably had the same look. We waited and waited, but nothing happened...no Bigfoot.

I'm not sure how long we sat there, but it seemed like an eternity. I was starting to think that maybe the beast wasn't going to show, but no sooner did I think that did we hear a noise near the trash cans. I whispered to the guys to get ready. I could feel my hands start to sweat as I held the net. Chunks and Jimmy started to shake, and Al's eyes were wide open. The noise by the trash cans continued. Then all of a sudden we heard a rushing on the trail. It sounded like whatever it was, it was closing in on us fast. Chunks said, "Oh, know there are two of them." Then before we knew it, a huge shadow was moving across the ground, and the beast was closing in. I said, "Guys, this is it...when I yell go, throw the net." The beast got closer, and I yelled, "Go!"

We all flung the net, and the beast ran right into it getting tangled and falling to the ground.

We then ran out and jumped on the hideous beast. We yelled and everyone came running out of the cabins to see what was going on. Someone turned on the outside lights, and we yelled we had the Bigfoot but there was another one by the trash. That's when we heard the beast say, "Get off me." I thought, Wait a minute, Bigfoot can't talk.

A FINAL SIGHTING

We jumped up and looked at the figure in the net struggling to get out. That's when we noticed the creature was wearing a Camp Daybreak t-shirt. It wasn't a big foot, it was Kyle and his shiny hair! "What are you guys doing?" he yelled. Chunks said, "We thought you were a Bigfoot!" Al looked at

Kyle and asked, "What in the world were you doing out here and running like you were?" Kyle stood up and brushed himself off and put his hat back on, you know the same one he always wears, and said, "I heard raccoons in the trash, and I was running over to scare them off so they won't make a mess." Kyle continued, "The whole Bigfoot story was just that...a story, I made it up. It was just a campfire story." I looked at him and asked, "So there's no monster?" Kyle let out a breath and said, "No, I never saw a Bigfoot, it was just a story to keep you guys in your beds, so I didn't have to chase you around all night." We all just stood there in silence and didn't say a word. Kyle smiled and told us all to go back to bed, and we all walked back into the cabin.

I looked at Chunks, and he was smiling. It was really odd he just kept smiling and then I noticed what he was smiling at. I looked at Jimmy, and I couldn't believe what I was seeing. Jimmy had peed his pants. He must have been so scared he couldn't hold it. Jimmy looked at us really ashamed, and we just smiled and said don't worry we won't tell a soul. Jimmy smiled, and Chunks yelled out, "Jimmy peed his pants!"

Everyone looked at Jimmy and laughed, and Jimmy said, "I get it."

I patted Jimmy on the back, and we all got right in our beds except for "Pee-pee Pants" Jimmy, which by the way became his new name for the next day or so. We went and changed then lay in his bed. Not long after, I fell asleep. I have to say, I was kind of disappointed that bigfoot wasn't real, but the good news was, the camp wasn't going to close. The rest of our time at Camp Daybreak flew by, and before I knew it, our parents were there picking us up. We said goodbye to all of our friends and Kyle. I got in the car with my dad. He asked me if I had fun, and I replied, "Yes, it was great!" We drove down the bumpy dirt road, and I could see the camp in the rearview mirror getting smaller and farther away as the mirror vibrated. That's when I noticed something out of the corner of my eye in the woods. It appeared to be really big. It looked at me as we drove past and turned and ran off. I couldn't believe my eyes...maybe Bigfoot was real. Maybe Kyle was wrong or hiding something. I looked at my dad who apparently didn't see what I saw, and thought,

I have to talk with Al and Chunks immediately!

AFTERWORD

Go to hangaripublishing.com to learn more about the Author and stay up to date with their newest releases.

www.ingramcontent.com/pod-product-compliance
Lightning Source LLC
Chambersburg PA
CBHW031300120626
46545CB00007B/2907